R. K. NARAYAN

R. K. NARAYAN

by

WILLIAM WALSH

Edited by Ian Scott-Kilvert

For my Wife:

this essay on a favourite writer

PUBLISHED FOR
THE BRITISH COUNCIL
BY LONGMAN GROUP LTD

LONGMAN GROUP LTD
Longman House, Burnt Mill, Harlow, Essex

*Associated companies, branches and
representatives throughout the world*

First published 1971
© William Walsh, 1971

*Printed in Great Britain by
F. Mildner & Sons, London, EC1R 5EJ*

SBN 0 582 01224 4

R. K. NARAYAN

R. K. NARAYAN is the senior and one of the most distinguished
novelists now writing in English in the Commonwealth.
Over a patient thirty years of composition he has built up a
devoted readership throughout the world from New York
to Moscow. His work is an original blend of Western
method and Eastern material, and he has succeeded in the
way that only a talent of the finest kind could in making an
Indian sensibility wholly at home in English art. And the
location of his novels, the Southern Indian town of Malgudi,
an imaginative version, one feels, of Narayan's beloved
Mysore, is as familiar to his readers as their own suburbs
and infinitely more interesting. The natural flavour of
Malgudi, Oriental and British, escapes like a scent from the
press of detail, and one comes to know the geography and
feel of the place as well as, and perhaps better than, one
knows one's own town. Malgudi's double provenance and
its twin character are impressed on the reader even by the
combination of names: the Kitson lamps and Vinayah
Mudali Street, Nallappa's Grove and Albert Mission College,
Kabir Street and Lawley Extension, the Mempi Hills and
the Board School, Malgudi Station and Krishna Medical
Hall: the soul of the East stained by pre-1914 England.

By now Narayan is the author of a substantial body of
fiction—ten novels and a number of short stories—all
remarkably even in the quality of its achievement. There is,
naturally enough, a more complex and introspective quality
in, say, *The Sweet-Vendor* (1967) than in his apprentice work,
Swami and Friends. I used to think the one exception to the
general high standard was *Mr Sampath* (1949) which treats
of the zany Indian film industry and which seemed to lack
something of the deftness and quiet assurance characteristic
of Narayan. I now believe that view to be wrong, as I shall
indicate later.

Narayan was born in 1907 in Madras of an old Brahmin
family. The family—they spoke Tamil at home—moved

3

early to Mysore where he learned his English in a small
school from one of those ferocious but by no means in-
efficient schoolmasters who appear in his fiction. His higher
education was at Maharaja's College, which is now part of
the University of Mysore, but he does not appear to have
made any mark as a scholar. His first book, *Swami and
Friends*, was published in 1935 and he has continued to
produce regularly ever since.

His novels are regional, in that they convey an intimate
sense of a given place, but not parochial. They include the
intimate resonance given by village life as well as the more
sophisticated tone of the impersonal city. He is much
preoccupied with the skills and problems of various kinds
of work, commerce, teaching, journalism, money-lending,
sweet-making. Within this scope, however, his habit is to
focus his attention sharply and to work from an instinct for
limitation. He writes of the middle class, his own class, the
members of which are neither too well off not to be worried
about money and position, nor dehumanized by absolute
need. His hero is usually modest, sensitive, ardent, wry about
himself and sufficiently conscious to have an active inner
life and to grope towards some existence independent of the
family. The family is the immediate context in which he
operates and his novels are remarkable for the delicacy and
precision of the family relations treated—that of son and
parents, and brother and brother in *The Bachelor of Arts;*
of husband and wife, and father and daughter in *The English
Teacher;* of father and son in *The Financial Expert;* of
grandmother and grandson in *Waiting for the Mahatma.*

The firmly delineated town, therefore, is the outer circle
of the action; within it is the subtler and more wavering
ring of the family; and at the centre of that stands, or rather
flinches, the Narayan hero, a tentative, spiritually sensitive,
appealingly limited character, in whom modesty is a
positive force, whether he be the leathery old proprietor of
a tiny industry like Jagan in *The Sweet-Vendor,* or the
converted con-man Raju in *The Guide* (apologetically

converted, note, in spite of himself), or the nervous editor of
the press on Market Road, Nataraj, in *The Man-Eater of
Malgudi*. The characteristic Narayan figure always has the
capacity to be surprised by the turn of events. His individuality has a certain formlessness, a lack of finish, indeed, as
though the definition of his personality depended upon the
play of external influences. Which of course in India, with
the immense weight of inherited tradition, it so frequently
does. This quality of the incompleteness in the person means
the further capacity not just to be startled by what happens
but to be at least in part reconstituted by it. The procedure
in a Narayan novel is almost invariably a renovation or
reforming of character in response to the encouragement or
provocation of events, which is never, however, total enough
to be revolutionary but sufficient to make a new bend in
the flow of continuity. If this is how the process appears to
the observer, it shows itself to the protagonist as his effort
to achieve a more explicit and articulate sense of self.

Narayan's novels are comedies of sadness, calling up the
name of Chekov, rather than anything in English literature,
as Graham Greene pointed out.[1] The sadness comes from
the painful experience of dismantling the routine self, which,
the context being Indian, seems less a private possession than
something distilled by powerful and ancient conventions,
and secondly the reconstitution, or more frequently, the
having reconstituted for one, of another personality. The
comedy arises from the sometimes bumbling, sometimes
desperate, sometimes absurd exploration of different
experience in the search for a new, and it may be, an exquisitely inappropriate, role. The complex theme of
Narayan's serious comedies, then, is—one must not burke
at the word in an Indian context—the rebirth of self and
the process of its pregnancy or education, the set of con-
ditions in which it takes place. Friction between the two
parts of the composition is prevented by a subtle oil of

---

[1] Introduction to *The Bachelor of Arts* (1937).

acceptance, secreted both by the inclusive and tolerant attitude of the author, and by what is in the end fundamentally an attitude of acceptance by the characters. These characters occupy a universe of which the substantial features are both the flux of being and the plurality of being. Things flow, an infinite variety of things, of men and manners, relations and women, avocations and degrees, joys, disappointments and disasters. To the author this is the nature of reality, to the characters what they will, perhaps, with a moderate kind of happiness, finally accommodate themselves to.

Malgudi, the locale of all the novels, is a metaphor of India. Whatever happens in the one happens in the other, but also, the reader begins to believe, whatever happens there happens everywhere. Against the background of a single place, and amid the utter variety of human kind, the single individual engages with the one, universal problem: the effort not just to be, but to become, human. The realization of this reading of experience is effected in the novels by means of a triple capacity in the author. First there is the minute fidelity with which the surface of Malgudi life is effortlessly reproduced, the streets, the houses, the shops, the temples, the trades, the routines and crises of the family, the exact grain and patina of place and people. Next, there is the author's unblurred perception of the complicated play of a whole throng of motives, each member of the group ousting another, and being replaced in turn, in even the simplest action. One of the most brilliant exhibitions of this gift for psychological and moral analysis occurs in *The Guide* in the way in which each thread of deception and sincerity is teased out by the author's nimble and tactful fingers. Accuracy of the surface is accompanied not only by this deftness of diagnosis but by a third quality, a subdued, suggested poetry, implicit in the natural relation Narayan finds between human actions and their purposes, understood or not, and the ancient, complex Indian myths. The orchestration of his work at this level adds another and more profound dimension to his perception. It exists at every point in his writing, whether in the central situation where the concept of rebirth is purely in the Indian tradition; or in the gorgeously comic renunciation of Jagan in *The Sweet-Vendor*, when he obeys the classical Indian prescription that 'in some stage in one's life one must uproot oneself from the accustomed surroundings and disappear so that others can continue in peace'; or, to give but one more of innumerable possible examples, in *The Man-Eater of Malgudi* where Vasu with 'the black halo of hair' becomes comprehensible, an element in a coherent situation, only when he is seen to be a 'Rakshasa', an active principle of destruction.

This complicated cargo is carried on an English style which is limpid, simple, calm and unaffected, natural in its run and tone, and beautifully measured to its purposes. It has neither the American purr of the combustion engine nor the thick marmalade quality of British English, and it communicates with complete ease a different, an Indian sensibility. When Narayan was in England in 1968 I asked him in a conversation on the radio[1] whether he found it any strain to write in English. His reply will interest the reader:

Until you mentioned another tongue I never had any idea that I was writing in another tongue. My whole education has been in English from the primary school, and most of my reading has been in the English language. The language and literature of this country flourished in the Indian soil until lately. It still remains a language of the intelligensia. But English has been with us for over a century and a half. I am particularly fond of the language. I was never aware that I was using a different, a foreign, language when I wrote in English, because it came to me very easily. I can't explain how. English is a very adaptable language. And it's so transparent it can take on the tint of any country.

Swami and Friends, Narayan's first book, is apparently a very slight affair, the account of a ten-year-old boy, his life at school and at home, his nicely discriminated friends, and the clutch of his schoolmasters, including the 'fire-eyed

[1] BBC, 23 February 1968.

Vedanayagan' and the effusively Christian Ebenezer. There is a touch of a Kipling boy in Swami (and perhaps there is something of Kipling's touch in the author), in his hectic adventures, his avidity for idleness, his horror at homework, his inauguration of the MCC in Malgudi, his misery in the examinations, his expulsion from two schools, his running away from home when things become intolerable. But the faintly patronizing glaze with which one can hardly help approaching the story of a normal boy, for all the fascination of the Indian context, begins to give way when one realizes that even in this earliest exercise the author is bringing to bear a mind very much more impressive than one would expect in the writer of a school story. It is not so much the boy's adventures, deliriously comic as they frequently are, which are being narrated but the boy's world which is being delicately established. The events have a certain conventional quality in them but even at the beginning of his work one sees that detached but re-morselessly observant eye of Narayan missing nothing and affectionately ridiculing stretches of human experience. His detachment enables him to allow the protagonist his freedom, what Henry James called 'respect for the liberty of the subject', so that there is a spontaneous, non-manipu-lated quality in the actions of Swami. And a boy at this period of his life is a remarkably attractive figure, competent in the way he conducts his life at home and school, whole and undistracted by money or sex, remarkably clear-eyed and both bold and sensitive. Swami is all this. At the same time he occupies the child's tilted and melodramatic universe in which all bonds have to be personal and in which neutrality is faintly menacing. He is an absolutist in being unable to conceive that things could be other than they are. He concentrates his energy in managing bumbling and intrusive adults.

'How many days is it since you have touched your books?' father asked as he blew off the fine layer of dust on Swaminathan's books, and

cleared the web that an industrious spider was weaving between a corner
of the table and the pile of books.

Swaminathan viewed this question as a gross breach of promise.

'Should I read even when I have no school?'

'Do you think you have passed the B.A.?' father asked.

'I mean, father, when the school is closed, when there is no examina-
tion, even then should I read?'

'What a question! You must read.'

'But, father, you said before the examinations that I needn't read after
they were over. Even Rajam does not read.' As he uttered the last
sentence, he tried to believe it; he clearly remembered Rajam's complain-
ing bitterly of a home-tutor who came and pestered him for two hours
a day thrice a week. Father was apparently deaf to Swaminathan's
remarks. He stood over Swaminathan and set him to dust his books and
clean his table. Swaminathan vigorously started blowing off the dust
from the book covers. He caught the spider carefully, and took it to the
window to throw it out. He held it outside the window and watched
it for a while. It was swinging from a strand that gleamed in a hundred
delicate tints.

'Look sharp! Do you want a whole day to throw out the spider?'
father asked. Swaminathan suddenly realised that he might have the
spider as his pet and that it would be a criminal waste to throw it out.
He secretly slipped it into his pocket and, after shaking an empty hand
outside the window, returned to his duty at the desk.

What is remarkable about this characteristic passage is not
so much the mirrored actuality of the facts as the luminous
insight into the boy's mind, the sense of the rhythm of his
wavering attention, the feeling for his tentative, not quite
smothered gesture of deception, the gift by which what
seems to be simply the author's external observation becomes
the occupancy of another's personality. Narayan's talent is
to be measured by the range of situation and character upon
which it can bring this gift to bear with a natural and un-
forced authority.

Look at the equal ease with which he reveals the boy's
terror as he runs away from home at night:

His ears became abnormally sensitive. They caught every noise his
feet made, with the slightest variations. His feet came down on the

ground with a light tick or a subdued crackle or a gentle swish, according to the object on the ground: small dry twigs, half-green leaves, or a thick layer of dry withered leaves. There were occasional patches of bare uncovered ground, and there the noise was a light thud, or pit pat; pit pat pit pat in monotonous repetition.

Or again, note the pointed precision with which the boy's father is shown giving his wife the news that he hasn't been able to find him:

> . . . he had assumed a heavy aggressive cheerfulness. . . . He tried to console her and rose to go out saying, again with a certain loud cheerfulness: 'I am going out to look for him. If he comes before I return, for Heaven's sake don't let him know what I am out for. I don't care to appear a fool in his eyes.'

This nimble, implacable, but quite unbitchy perception of human psychology is immediately evident at the beginning of *The Bachelor of Arts*, published in 1937, where we see a writer fully arrived and wholly at ease with his manner and his material. The first words, drawing a light, precise line without smudge or haze, define the area to be treated and the nature of the subject:

> Chandran was just climbing the steps of the College Union when Natesan, the secretary, sprang on him and said, 'You are just the person I was looking for. You remember your old promise?'
> 'No,' said Chandran promptly, to be on the safe side.

We catch immediately the tone of the undergraduates' concerns in Albert Mission College, the Cambridge of Malgudi, at once desperately urgent and absurdly inappropriate not just to life in a serious, heavy-bottomed way, but to anything at all. At the same time we sense the flavour of Chandran's personality: tender, tense, sharp, self-protective, unformed. Chandran's two worlds, college and home, chime in contrast and agreement. In one, life is cerebral and relationships intense but fundamentally indifferent; in the other life is instinctive and shut-in, and relationships are intimate and relaxed. Each part of the composition points up the other: on one side the angular dons humming with abstract passion about the incompetence of Bradley or the necessity for inaugurating an Historical Society at the College, without which, it seems, society and history itself would crumble away; on the other side the distinct temperaments of the family, dry, generous father, bustling, grumpy mother, small brother and pampered Chandran, rubbing against each other in innumerable tiny irritations—but united by and safe in a basic serenity.

I use the term 'composition' deliberately because the simplicity of Narayan's narrative line, in which each event glides smoothly into the next in an apparently straightforward and realistic way, tends to mask the real if subdued subtlety of the structure. The second, the balancing part of the novel, leads out from home and then from college, which Chandran leaves, after graduating, 'tender and depressed'. It includes first, Chandran's love affair with Malathi, an ecstasy of one-sided, idealistic tenderness, and secondly, a bewitching account, bantering, accurate, tender, of the intricate absurdities of the Indian marriage system. When the marriage plan collapses after colliding with an unfavourable horoscope, Chandran is distracted. He leaves home, has a bout of slightly hysterical, non-intoxicated dissipation in Madras, with the odd, middle-aged Kailas, and disappears in the role of a wandering holy-man, which is for Chandran a form of mild and painless suicide fitted to his anguished, timid spirit. It is in keeping, too, with the profoundly tolerant and gentle feeling of the novel, where even incisive perception into character is humorous and forgiving, and appropriate in the Indian way also, that Chandran should have his moment of realization under a banyan tree in a remote village at the foot of a range of mountains:

The night had fallen. Somebody had brought and left a lighted lantern beside him. He looked about. They had all brought gifts for him, milk and fruits and food. The sight of the gifts sent a spear through his heart. He felt a cad, a fraud, and a confidence trickster. These were gifts for a counterfeit exchange. He wished that he deserved their faith in him.

The sight of the gifts made him unhappy. He ate some fruit and drank a little milk with the greatest self-deprecation.

He moved away from the gifts; still the light shone on them. He even blew out the lantern—he did not deserve the light.

This moment is the high point of awareness for Chandran, but a nature so light and febrile cannot sustain this cold condition and he returns, as he was bound to, to the warmth of the family and the comforting huddle of Malgudi life, sacrificing the prospect of a European education offered by his father, finding with his father's help a job as a collector of newspaper subscriptions as well as another girl, appropriately fair, well-connected, and most important of all possessed of a propitious horoscope. To graduate to a very ordinary stability was the most the Bachelor of Arts could hope for, but the fleeting logic of his transformation, a logic both of personality and of circumstance, is fixed with delicate authority and complete conviction.

In one of his periods of agitated self-analysis, Chandran describes his aim to achieve 'a life freed from distracting illusions and hysterics'. This was a huge ambition for so evanescent a character. It is an apter description of Krishnan in *The English Teacher*, published in 1945. His is a less-brittle, more complex personality. He is a 100-rupee-a-month lecturer in English in the same college who lives apart from his wife and daughter in a college hostel, who does not hide the asperity of his reactions to many of his colleagues, and whose earlier idealism for his subject and his students is rapidly turning sandy. 'What tie was there between me and them? Did I absorb their personalities as did the old masters and merge them in mine? I was merely a man who had mugged earlier than they the introduction and the notes in the Verity edition of *Lear*, and guided them through the mazes of Elizabethan English.' The reality of Krishnan's generous, self-centred, sceptical personality is established in Narayan's oblique, self-effacing way by a technique of the lightest touches, each one a fleck of gaiety and the crispest insight. Krishnan is a highly intelligent man and he had expected to find the theme of his life in the intellectual world, but everything, his teaching, his thought, his poetry, left him cloudily dissatisfied, full of 'a vague disaffection, a self-rebellion . . . always leaving behind a sense of something missing'. A letter from his father breaks into his brooding discontent to announce that his wife and daughter are coming to live with him and to ask him to find a house for them. This letter inaugurates the next part of Krishnan's life in which he lives with his wife and daughter in their queer little house in Sarayu Street, rented from a peculiar, impressive, shrunken old miser. 'Are you the owner of the house?' 'No', he replied, promptly, in his querulous voice. 'God is the owner and I am his slave.' The growth and realization of Krishnan's love for his wife and child is lyrically alive and alight, the feeling just, true and controlled. Krishnan rejoins the world of the particular, of specific feeling, genuine response, significant tradition. The meaning of life becomes densely present and actual to him. His collapse when his wife dies after a lingering, misdiagnosed illness, caught on a visit to a new and grander house, is total.

The second part of the novel supply plaits together the two themes of Krishnan's growing devotion to his tiny daughter and his effort to recreate his connexion with his dead wife. The first subject, so full of invitations to senti-mental disaster, is dealt with in a feeling but wholly un-sentimental way. The child, who has in her miniature personality something of the dry directness of her mother and her grandmother, becomes all the time a more firmly evoked and individual presence. Her vivid being, her tiny, brilliant mirroring of her mother's temperament painfully intensifies the sense of the mother's absence, but, paradoxi-cally, by a creative tension, keeps her identity from dying away. In a feat unprecedented in realistic fiction, out of a kind of tranquil audacity, Narayan succeeds in his second theme in persuading the reader to accept Krishnan's efforts through the agency of an amiable, homely medium—and not only his efforts but his success—to regain touch with his wife. Through the medium's reports, and then through Krishnan's own capacity to register it, the wife's refracted presence becomes more and more active until in the end Krishnan and she meet again in a moment of illumination, an experience of absolute openness, presence and communion:

> We stood at the window, gazing on a slender, red streak over the eastern rim of the earth. A cool breeze lapped our faces. The boundaries of our personalities suddenly dissolved. It was a moment of rare, immutable joy—a moment for which one feels grateful to Life and Death.

This moment of union, of perfection, contrasts with the harder, leaner reflection of Krishnan a little earlier in the novel when visiting his ancestral village, '. . . the fact must be recognized. A profound unmitigated loneliness is the only truth of life.' The intensity of this formulation belongs to a certain character at a particulaɪ point in the novel where indeed its strength of feeling helps to explain the extraordinary efforts Krishnan makes to regain his connexion with his dead wife. But the sense of it is one of the deep, constitutive intuitions of Narayan's fiction, giving gravity and depth to the rippling liveliness of the humour. We see it in Raju in *The Guide* (1958), standing utterly alone like a stone among the waves of people; in a less profound way, as a more ordinary loneliness, we find it at the beginning of *Waiting for the Mahatma* (1955) when Sriram and his grandmother are celebrating his twentieth birthday:

> So all alone next day he celebrated his twentieth birthday. His guest as well as hostess was his grandmother. No one outside could have guessed what an important occasion was being celebrated in that house in Kabir Street numbered '14'. The house was over two hundred years old and looked it. It was the last house in the street, or 'the first house' as his great-grandfather used to say at the time he built it. From here one saw the backs of market buildings and heard night and day the babble of the big crowd moving on the market road.

The opposition of shuffling multitude and solitary individual is part of that muted dialectic which sustains the

world of Narayan's novels. The sense of the faceless,
deprived mass is particularly suitable in *Waiting for the
Mahatma*, where politics in the shape of Gandhi's Quit
India campaign provide the context in which the light-
weight Sriram stumbles his uncomprehending way towards
adulthood. (Not that this is a political novel: the politics
are just one of the facts of the case, no more.) The situation
is a classical one in Narayan. Sriram, an orphan—his mother
died delivering him, his father was killed in Mesopotamia—
lives with his formidable grannie who has month by month
banked his father's pension in the Fund Office and who now
at his twentieth birthday solemnly transfers to him the
'brown calico-bound passbook'. Sriram is uneasily conscious
of the pointlessness of his life, cossetted as it is by layers of
custom and female devotion. He is awakened out of his
discontented trance by the beautiful young woman collect-
ing for Gandhi, who turns out to be a protegé of the Master
and indeed in temperament almost a projection of the saint
himself, so that Gandhi who appears only intermittently is,
by means of this girl, indirectly present throughout the
novel. Sriram understands the Gandhian doctrine and the
girl's interpretation of it only in his own egotistic and
short-sighted manner. He becomes a clumsy follower and
then a romantic small-scale terrorist. He is captured, released
and achieves just that degree of responsibility he is capable
of, which in his case is one of acceptance and stability and
submission to the stronger character of the young woman,
Bharati.

For the first time these many months and years he had a free and
happy mind, a mind without friction and sorrow of any kind. No
hankering for a future or regret for a past. This was the first time in his
life that he was completely at peace with himself, satisfied profoundly
with existence itself. The very fact that one was breathing, feeling, and
seeing, seemed sufficient matter for satisfaction now.

Waiting for the Mahatma like all Narayan's novels is remarkable for the richness and variety of its minor characters.

The swiftest notation summons into being the gruff and superbly vigorous grannie, whose vitality is such that lying on her bier, in readiness to be burnt, her toes twitch and she has to be dragged off, revived and sent off to Benares for a future of continuing vigour and acerbity. Or Narayan can with a flick suggest the suave and peace-loving manager of the Fund Office or the friendly rogue Kanni, the shop-keeper, cowing his credit-demanding clientele: 'What do you think I am! How dare you come again without cash? You think you can do me in? You are mistaken. I can swallow ten of you at the same time, remember'. Or he can in a half dozen pages, almost as much by omission as by what he puts in, make a living portrait of the half sinister, half clownish revolutionary photographer Jagadish, who sees himself as 'the chief architect of independent India, the chief operator in ejecting the British', and who has assembled numerous albums of photographs to prove it.

But the more profound comedy of *Waiting for the Mahatma*, more profound because mixed with sadness and disappointment, is provided by the gap between absurd or stupid or merely human failures and the simplicity of the portrait of Gandhi. It is a picture drawn without a single pretentious or false gesture. The genius of the Mahatma is shown to be the most exquisite, the purest, the most incandescent honesty and common sense. He is a man (or perhaps he is a God) naked to reality whose values are utterly transparent, and he also has that quality of curious, un-sentimental dryness Narayan appears to attribute to those he admires most, perhaps because its astringency is a correc-tive to the national inclination towards the wambling and ineffable.

A characteristic, indeed pretty well an habitual, device of Narayan is to introduce somewhere in the novel often in a minor role, some densely enigmatic character, out of a conviction it would seem, that certain experiences, certain events or people, like knots in wood, are discontinuous with ordinary life and impervious to the usual intellectual tools. One such is the ancient landlord in *The English Teacher* or the middle-aged Madras rake in *The Bachelor of Arts* or the strange priest in *The Financial Expert*. Sometimes the character may be kindly like the amiable medium in *The English Teacher*, or malevolent like the icily sinister Marko in *The Guide*. The office of these characters is to demonstrate, in keeping with Narayan's profoundly Indian and religious view of life, the inexplicable in experience, the human capacity for not being wholly susceptible to rational analysis. The singular thing about *Mr Sampath* is that it brings this normally subordinate character into the centre of the action. Indeed, the body of the novel is made up of the relations between the baffling Mr Sampath and the all too comprehensible Srinivas, first as printer in an obscure establishment to Srinivas's editor in the production of a paper, *The Banner*, and secondly as an Indian Cecil B. de Mille to Srinivas's scriptwriter in the production of an Indian film epic. There is a neat reversal here, master modifying into servant, servant into master. This dialectical swing qualifies all the commerce of the two. Mr Sampath at first appears as decisive and efficient, Srinivas harassed and becalmed, so that even 'the question of a career seemed to him as embarrassing as a physiological detail . . . agriculture, apprenticeship in a bank, teaching, law. He gave everything a trial once.' This is not a novel in which in any Western way characters are transformed by some inner energy. Srinivas is already a formed personality at the beginning of the novel. Rather, Narayan's fiction proceeds by revealing the manifold, contradictory nature of personality and existence. We see the same people from different points of view and therefore see the differences *in* them, the contrary, coexisting layers of being. No one of these identities is in any bleakly protestant way the 'true' one, since all are equally true and equally illusory.

Only the 'swift and continuous movement of time, the ruthlessness of its flow' is constant and unmistakable. And since we are not simply metaphysical beings but human

creatures encased in flesh, one of the protections from the
oppression of time is things, palpable, physical things,
particularly those hallowed by use and custom which have,
as it were, the goodwill of time, like 'the steel pen with a
fat green wooden handle' belonging to Krishnan's father in
The English Teacher, or Nataraj's 'roll-topped desk supported
on bow legs with ivy vines carved on them' in *The Man-
Eater of Malgudi*, or Jagan's chair in *The Sweet-Vendor*—
'nearly a century old, with shiny brass strips on the arms
and back and legs'. The finest example of the preserving
sanity of objects and of an art which is above all the re-
constructing of the concrete inviting the reader to an im-
mersion in the particular, comes in fact in *Mr Sampath*.
(And how silly and frivolous words like superstition appear
in this context):

He prayed for a moment before a small image of Nataraja which
his grandmother had given him when he was a boy. This was one of the
possessions he had valued most for years. It seemed to be a refuge from
the oppression of time. It was of sandal wood, which had deepened a
darker shade with years, just four inches high. The carving represented
Nataraja with one foot raised and one foot pressing down a demon, his
four arms outstretched, with his hair flying, the eyes rapt in contempla-
tion, an exquisitely poised figure. His grandmother had given it to him
on his eighth birthday. She had got it from her father, who discovered
it in a packet of saffron they had brought from the shop on a certain day.
It had never left Srinivas since that birthday. It was on his own table at
home, or in the hostel, wherever he might be. It had become a part of
him, this little image. He often sat before it, contemplated its proportions,
and addressed it thus: 'Oh, God, you are trampling a demon under your
foot, and you show us a rhythm, though you appear to be still. I grasp
the symbol but vaguely. You hold a flare in your hand. May a ray of that
light illumine my mind!' He silently addressed it thus. It had been his
first duty for decades now. He never started his day without spending
a few minutes before this image.

'You show us a rhythm.' Perhaps this is the essential
achievement of Narayan's fiction. It shows us a rhythm,
the inimitable, unfakeable rhythm of feeling, intelligence

and life. This rhythm shows its fullest and most varied movement in four novels representing the ripest in Narayan's mature art, *The Financial Expert, The Guide, The Man-Eater of Malgudi* and *The Sweet-Vendor*. I have written elsewhere in detail on three of these novels and I hope I may be forgiven if I direct the reader's attention there for a treatment fuller than I have space for here.[1]

There is a marvellous scene in *Mr Sampath*, the pure milk of gaiety, in which garlanded priests, 'with their foreheads stamped with ash and vermilion, and their backs covered with hand-spun long wraps' dedicate to the Gods (but as Narayan pointedly observes, for gifts in cash and kind) Mr Sampath's third-rate studio for the production of a fifth-rate epic, applying a millenial poetic ritual to one of the sleaziest examples of modernity. 'A few minutes before the appointed moment they rose, lit the camphor, and circled the flame before the Gods, sounding a bell. Then they went to the camera and stuck a string of jasmine and a dot of sandal paste on it.' Much of the comedy of *The Financial Expert* (1952) which includes in Margayya probably Narayan's greatest single comic creation, comes from this friction of discrepancies. The clashing of contrasting orders of experience, each probing and placing the other, generates a distinct and buoyant kind of comedy. The action of *The Financial Expert* moves from petty huckstering and village money-lending outside the doors of the local Co-operative Land Mortgage Bank, with Margayya humiliated by the abuse not only of the manager but of the bank's peon for illegally extracting loan forms, to the sophisticated world of capital movements—a contrast, however, which in keeping with Narayan's view of the fundamental oneness of existence, is also a continuity. The one substance of money appears in different guises. But *The Financial Expert* is no simple story of success, from door-keeper to director.

[1] For *The Guide*, cf. *A Human Idiom*, 1964; for *The Man-Eater of Malgudi* and *The Sweet-Vendor*, cf. *A Manifold Voice*, 1970.

Margayya will do anything for money, even to being religious for it. He moves from rags to riches, from a cotton to a lace dhoti, not really by financial astuteness at all but by obeying the mystifying injunction of the priest in the local temple and by performing elaborate rituals for forty days to the Goddess Lakshmi, the Goddess of Wealth:

. . . 'That means you should propitiate Goddess Lakshmi, the Goddess of Wealth. When she throws a glance and it falls on someone, he becomes rich, he becomes prosperous, he is treated by the world as an eminent man, his words are treated as something of importance. All this you seem to want.'

'Yes,' said Margayya authoritatively. 'Why not?'

Why not indeed? He falls in with the weird Dr Pal who has composed a modern *Kama-Sutra*, entitled 'Bed Life or the Science of Marital Happiness'. Margayya buys it on a dare for the contents of his purse, goes into partnership with Mr Lal to publish it under the more respectable title of 'Domestic Harmony' and makes his fortune.

The collision of opposites is seen again in Margayya's attitude to money. This mean, servile, bullying man will do anything for money, anything. But when he has it it becomes not a sordid medium of exchange, but a pure, awesome abstraction, a godhead to be worshipped: 'Riches any hard-working fool could attain by some watchfulness, while acquiring wealth was an extraordinarily specialized job. It came to persons who had on them the grace of the Goddess fully and who could use their wits.' Money produces a mystic feeling in Margayya which causes him to live in a sort of radiance. As suddenly as money comes, as suddenly it goes, again through the intervention of Dr Pal, who sets about rumours to damage Margayya's credit. But Margayya is not converted or refined by his reduction to penury. His last act is to set his son on the precise path he has taken himself. *He* has not changed. The Goddess once smiled on him, now she frowns. He and life are just the same.

Narayan is no simple humorist and his comedy is so

effective, piercing as well as amusing, because the humour is part, a coherent part, of a more inclusive vision which is ultimately sad, informed as it is by a sense of the transience and illusion of human action. The humour is also part of a gifted novelist's full technique for treating human reality. In *The Financial Expert* we see the artist's fresh and complex discernment which can fix not only the comic, but the frayed and driven, self of Margayya, and simultaneously evoke that other part of individuality which we have in relationships: in Margayya's case, in his relationships with his soured wife, his spoilt son, his brow-beaten office worker, with his son's oppressed teachers, with the peasants and business men, with the menacing sociologist Dr Pal, and the hearty, obtuse businessman, Mr Lal.

Just as *The Financial Expert* can be interpreted as a commentary on the dealings of the Goddess Lakshmi with one of her devotees, or perhaps as an account of a quarrel between her and the Goddess Saraswathi, the deity presiding over knowledge and enlightenment, so the meticulously executed surface, as in the other novels, is disturbed by the faint resonance of an ancient Indian myth. The poetry insinuates itself into the documentary. *The Guide*, which may well be the greatest of Narayan's novels, retells the famous Indian story of the confidence man who becomes, in spite of himself, at the pushing of the Gods, the man deserving of trust; *The Man-Eater of Malgudi*, in the person of Vasu, embodies the myth of a ferocious inimical spirit, the 'Rakshasa', who carries within himself, unknown to himself, a tiny seed of self-destruction. ('Otherwise what is to happen to humanity?' as one of the hero's friends observes.) *The Sweet-Vendor* rehearses yet again the Indian doctrine of the renunciation of the world (although Jagan the elderly sweet-maker who feels that 'at some stage in one's life one must uproot oneself from the accustomed surroundings and disappear so that others can continue in peace', 'disappears' accompanied in a prudent, business-like way, by his cheque book). I have spoken of retelling and rehearsing, but of course the poetic myth exists only as a faint, subterranean murmur. It signals remotely or hints obscurely at the approval or the disavowel of the Gods, of life, as in this scene at the end of *The Guide*, in which Raju, ex-gaolbird, ex-tour-courier, ex-theatrical agent, ex-almost anything, dies fasting on behalf of the peasants who, in their need for rain, have wished on him his role of saint.

At five-thirty in the morning, the doctors examined the Swami. They wrote and signed a bulletin saying: 'Swami's condition grave. Declines glucose and saline. Should break the fast immediately. Advise procedure.' They sent a man running to send off this telegram to their headquarters.

It was a top priority government telegram, and it fetched a reply within an hour. 'Imperative that Swami should be saved. Persuade best to co-operate. Should not risk life. Try give glucose and saline. Persuade Swami resume fast later'.

They sat beside the Swami and read to him the message. He smiled at it. He beckoned Velan to come nearer.

The doctors appealed, 'Tell him he should save himself. Please do your best. He is very weak.'

Velan bent close to the Swami and said, 'The doctors say—'.

In answer Raju asked the man to bend nearer, and whispered, 'Help me to my feet,' and clung to his arm and lifted himself. He got up to his feet. He had to be held by Velan and another on each side. In the profoundest silence the crowd followed him down. Everyone followed at a solemn, silent pace. The eastern sky was red. Many in the camp were still sleeping. Raju could not walk, but he insisted upon pulling himself along all the same. He panted with the effort. He went down the steps of the river, halting for breath on each step, and finally reached his basin of water. He stepped into it, shut his eyes, and turned towards the mountain, his lips muttering the prayer. Velan and another held him each by an arm. The morning sun was out by now; a great shaft of light illuminated the surroundings. It was difficult to hold Raju on his feet, as he had a tendency to flop down. They held him as if he were a baby. Raju opened his eyes, looked about, and said, 'Velan, it's raining in the hills. I can feel it coming up under my feet, up my legs—' He sagged down.

Not only does this final scene in *The Guide*, a novel which explores the intricate, folded terrain of sincerity and self-deception, display Narayan's restrained poetic gift, not only does it exhibit his creative accuracy of notation—the activity of the crowd just before is registered with minutely particularized fidelity—it also, like many other scenes in many other novels, reveals that psychological acumen which constantly surprises and illumines the reader. Raju is where he is, martyr instead of con-man, because he is incapable of wounding the peasants who see him as a holy man. He cannot refuse the wishes of others for him. He is obeying that law by which our natures are largely constituted by the expectations of others.

But each of us also has, as Coleridge noted,[1] an equally strong instinct 'not to suffer any one form to pass into me and to become a usurping self'; a fierce instinct to preserve the shape of our own identity. There is a brilliant example—no, not an example, an embodiment—of this intuition in *The Financial Expert*. Margayya is distraught at the reported death of his son. There is chaos in the home and his estranged brother-in-law and his family appear on the scene in the crisis. And what does Margayya feel? He is shocked that the hallowed routine of hostility is to be disrupted:

Through all his grief a ridiculous question (addressed to his brother) kept coming to his mind: 'Are we friends now—no longer enemies? What about our feud?' A part of his mind kept wondering how they could live as friends, but the numerous problems connected with this seemed insoluble. 'We had got used to this kind of life. Now I suppose we shall have to visit each other and enquire and so on . . .' All that seemed to be impossible to do. He wished to tell him then and there: 'Don't let this become an excuse to change our present relationship.'

Narayan's fastidious art, blending exact realism, poetry, melancholy, perception and gaiety, is without precedent in English literature, and as far as one can see, without following. It is engaging because of the charm and authenticity of its Indian setting, moving because of the substantial, universal human nature which it incarnates. And it carries

[1] cf. *Inquiring Spirit*, edited by K. Coburn, 1951, p. 68.

with it at every point a species of humour as appealing and homely as freckles on the skin. Perhaps this humour is its deepest wisdom, the 'fault' in a geological sense, conveying its unique individuality and communicating a sense, crisp and unrebellious, of human limitation. In Narayan's latest novel, *The Sweet-Vendor*, there is a meeting in an overgrown garden between Jagan and a stone carver, one of those significant encounters used by Narayan to propel the action forward, in the course of which the sculptor reminisces for a moment; his tiny story, in its tone, phrasing and quiet *finesse*, conveys exactly the idiom of this most individual of sensibilities; and it offers, too, a small, lucid image of Narayan's belief in the mysterious balance of life contributed by human fallibility. 'I always remember the story of the dancing figure of Nataraj, which was so perfect that it began a cosmic dance and the town itself shook as if an earthquake had rocked it, until a small finger on the figure was chipped off. We always do it; no one ever notices it, but we always create a small flaw in every image; it's for safety.'

R. K. NARAYAN

A Select Bibliography

(Place of publication London, unless stated otherwise)

Separate Works:

SWAMI AND FRIENDS (1935). *Novel*

THE BACHELOR OF ARTS: A novel (1937).

THE DARK ROOM: A novel (1938).

MALGUDI DAYS (1941). *Short Stories*

DODU, AND OTHER STORIES; Mysore [1943]

CYCLONE, AND OTHER STORIES (1944).

THE ENGLISH TEACHER (1945). *Novel*

—issued in USA in 1953 under the title *Grateful to Life and Death.*

AN ASTROLOGER'S DAY, AND OTHER STORIES (1947).

MR SAMPATH (1949) *Novel*

—issued in USA in 1957 under the title *The Printer of Malgudi.*

THE FINANCIAL EXPERT: A novel (1952).

WAITING FOR THE MAHATMA: A novel (1955).

LAWLEY ROAD: Thirty-two short stories (1956).

THE GUIDE (1958). *Novel*

SUNDAY: Sketches and Essays (1960).

MY DATELESS DIARY; Mysore (1960). *Essays*

THE MAN-EATER OF MALGUDI (1962). *Novel*

GODS, DEMONS AND OTHERS (1965). *Short Stories*

THE SWEET-VENDOR (1967). *Novel*

FICTION AND THE READING PUBLIC IN INDIA, ed. C. D. Narasimhaiah; Mysore (1967)

—contains an article by Narayan entitled 'The World of the Story-teller'.

A HORSE AND TWO GOATS, AND OTHER STORIES (1970).

Critical Studies:

INDO-ANGLIAN LITERATURE, by K. R. S. Iyengar; Bombay (1943).

THE INDIAN CONTRIBUTION TO ENGLISH LITERATURE, by K. R. S. Iyengar; Bombay (1945).

'The Intricate Alliance: the Novels of R. K. Narayan', by W. Walsh, *Review of English Literature*, II, iv, October 1961.

'Sweet Mangoes and Malt Vinegar: Novels of R. K. Narayan', by W. Walsh, *The Listener*, 1 March 1962.

INDIAN WRITING IN ENGLISH, by K. R. S. Iyengar (1962).

A HUMAN IDIOM: LITERATURE AND HUMANITY by W. Walsh (1964).

'Nataraja and the Packet of Saffron', by W. Walsh, *Encounter*, October 1964.

'Literature in Malaysia', by T. Wigneson, *The Journal of Commonwealth Literature*, No. 2, December 1966.

FICTION AND THE READING PUBLIC IN INDIA, by C. D. Narasimhaiah; Mysore (1967).

THE WRITER'S GANDHI, by C. D. Narasimhaiah; Patiala (1967).

'R. K. Narayan's *Grateful to Life and Death*', by S. C. Harrex, *The Literary Criterion*, VIII, iii, Winter 1968.

INDO-ANGLIAN FICTION, by P. P. Mehta; Bareilly (1968).

CRITICAL ESSAYS ON INDIAN WRITING IN ENGLISH, ed. M. K. Nail, S. K. Desai and G. S. Amur; Dharwar, 1968.

'Indian Writing in English: An Introduction', by C. D. Narasimhaiah, *The Journal of Commonwealth Literature*, No. 5, July 1968.

'The Art of R. K. Narayan', by V. Panduranga Rao, *The Journal of Commonwealth Literature*, No. 5, July 1968.

'The Short Stories of R. K. Narayan', by Perry D. Westbrook, *The Journal of Commonwealth Literature*, No. 5, July 1968.

THE SWAN AND THE EAGLE; Simla (1969)
—contains a chapter 'R. K. Narayan: The Comic as a mode of study in maturity', by C. D. Narasimhaiah.

'The Indian Short Story in English: A Survey', by C. V. Venugopal, *The Banasthali Patrika*, 12, January 1969.

'Problems of the Indian Novelist in English', by C. P. Verghese, *The Banasthali Patrika*, 12, January 1969.

'Renaissance in Indo-Anglian Literature', by C. Karnani, *The Banasthali Patrika*, 13, July 1969.

'Old Places, Old Faces, Old Tunes: A critical study of R. K. Narayan's latest fiction', by T. Malhotra, *The Banasthali Patrika*, 13, July 1969.

'Some aspects of the Literary Development of R. K. Narayan', by N. Mukerji, *The Banasthali Patrika*, 13, July 1969.

'R. K. Narayan's Novels: Acceptance of life', by K. Venkatachari, *Osmania Journal of English Studies*, VII, 1, 1970.

INDIAN WRITING IN ENGLISH: CRITICAL ESSAYS, by D. McCutchion: Calcutta (1970).

A MANIFOLD VOICE: STUDIES IN COMMONWEALTH LITERATURE, by W. Walsh (1970).

JOHN IS EASY TO PLEASE, by Ved Mehta (1971)
—contains two essays on Narayan.

WRITERS AND THEIR WORK